Ruby Luna's Moontime

TESSA VENUTI SANDERSON

Ruby Luna's Moontime *by Tessa Venuti Sanderson*

Text and illustration copyright ©2019 Tessa Venuti Sanderson
Published by Castenetto & Co.
All rights reserved.

No part of this book may be produced in any form without permission from the publisher.

Library of Congress cataloguing-in-publication data available.

ISBN 978-0-9933751-5-6

Manufactured by *KDP*.
Layout and design: *Emy Farella*

This book is dedicated to all the women who've shared their stories of their first period with me; Anna, Rosie, Ellie and Neela who gave me feedback; and to the tween Tessa who would have loved this book. May my daughters Zara and Alma have a smooth journey through their menarche one day.

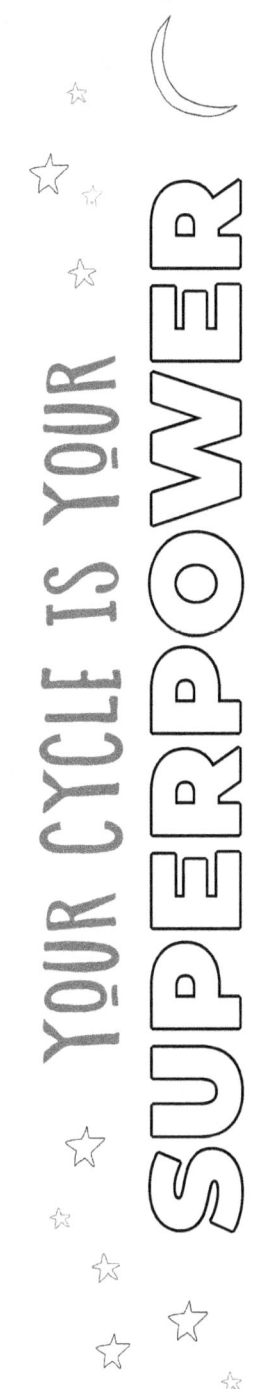

Cut this bookmark out & colour in

Chapters

1 - Shh! Don't tell..7

2 - Disaster strikes...30

3 - What's your favourite season?.................48

4 - Butterflies in the heart...............................67

5 - Endings & Beginnings...............................80

6 - Rollercoaster feelings................................99

7 - My secret superpower.............................111

1
Shh! Don't tell...

9th February DAY 1

I'm Ruby Luna and I'm ten years old. I have a little brother, Dante, who's seven and an older half-sister who lives in Italy. She's 19. I don't have a pet, but I would love to have a pug dog.

I can't wait to see my half-sister Rose (her real name is Rosalind like my grandma, but she says people only use that name when they're cross with her!!). The reason I can't wait to see her is that I have had something HUGE happen and only my mum and dad, and my two best friends know. My best friends are both called Beth and so in our house we call them Beth One and Beth Two (or Beth B and Beth F) so we know who we're talking about.

The two Beths were excited to be told my secret (I rang them up especially) but I don't think they really understood what I was talking about. They haven't started yet after all. And they don't have older sisters who have started their periods. Oops, didn't mean to write that yet, on the first page!! Yes, dear Diary I have started my period.

I woke up in the morning and when I got out of bed, I noticed blood on my leg. My mum had talked to me about periods a while ago coz she said she could see that my body was changing. I'm a whole head taller than most girls in my class and I'm curvier. That's what she said: curvier. I was worried I was getting a teeny bit fat, but mum said it's normal to get wider hips as you grow up. She said I'm perfect the way I am. She says that a lot, which is kind of nice and kind of annoying too.

So anyway, I got out of bed and saw the blood. At first, I was confused and thought how did a nosebleed get all the way down there? And then it clicked! My first period!! I was excited and nervous at the same time. I got some toilet paper from the bathroom and wiped up the blood on my leg, but then saw it was on my sheet so I called out to mum to come. She shouted back "Just a second" like she always does, but after five minutes she actually came in through the doorway.

She looked surprised when she saw the blood on the sheet, with her mouth in an "O" shape, and then ran over and gave me a big hug. She just ignored the blood on the sheet and kept squeezing me until I had to tell her to stop. She actually had a tear in her eye! She's so emotional. I pointed to the sheet and she pulled the duvet off the top of the bed and put that on the floor. Then she gathered together the sheet and said she would soak it in cold water, so it didn't stain.

I was very happy she was taking care of it. I don't think I will want to do that if I have daughters one day! She came running back up the stairs and started flapping around the bathroom looking for pads. She doesn't use pads: she prefers a cup thing. The first time I saw it in the bathroom, I picked it up because I didn't know what it was for. When I realised, I dropped it on the floor!

She found some pads with wings for me and tried to show me how to put them in my knickers, but I already know because I tried it out at a friend's house once. We found her mum's pads in the bathroom and took the strip off the back to stick it in our knickers. It got stuck to our legs and we couldn't stop laughing. Mum said she'll get some reusable pads for me to try because they'll be better for the environment.

10th February   DAY 2

I'm glad my period started on the Saturday because I stayed all morning on the sofa. I felt ok when I first got up and then after breakfast I just wanted to lay down and cuddle a hot water bottle. My body felt achy and heavy, a bit lower down than my tummy. In the afternoon, my mum got me to have a walk to the shops and back to get some milk and that helped a bit.

In the evening, my mum came into my room and said she had something to give me. I thought it was going to be some more pads! But she gave me a little box and when I opened it up there was a really lovely necklace with a pendant with glimmering shell. I think it's called mother of pearl or something. She said it was to mark my first period. It's kind of funny to get a present for starting your period. I don't think I got one for having my first poo. Anyway, it is really nice. She said I was just starting on the journey to becoming a woman, but at 10 years old I don't feel anywhere near to feeling like a grown up.

Then after dinner, I went back up to my bedroom to get changed into my pjs and there was an envelope on my pillow. I thought it was something else from my mum because she always puts little notes in my lunch box. Things like "love you to the moon and back" or "you are a great person". But NO!!! It was a card from my dad saying "I hear you got your first period. Well done!". That made me laugh. A LOT. I think probably my mum said he had to do something. I bet she even bought the card. I've tucked it in the back of this diary because I don't want my brother to get hold of it.

Today, I've gone through four pads. Not that they were full or anything, but I was a bit paranoid of the blood leaking through. I didn't have tummy ache today and was super hungry.

11th February   DAY 3

Yesterday mum asked me if she could tell the teacher about my period starting in case I needed any help. I thought that was super embarrassing, but Miss Peters is really nice and so I said ok in the end.

I felt really nervous about going to school with the pads in my bag. I'm getting quicker at changing them, but they make a noise when you're pulling the strip off the back or scrunching up the wrapper. My mum said not to put the pads down the toilet, but there are no bins in the toilet cubicle at school. I put the pads rolled up back in my rucksack, inside the bag my mum gave me. I didn't know what else to do with them.

When I got home, I didn't tell mum straight away. I don't know why. I didn't think she'd be cross with me, but something stopped me. I put the rolled-up pads in the bin at home, but mum must have seen them. She said "That's a lot of pads. Have you been bleeding a lot?" I told her that it was not just from the time I got home but from the whole day. So the story came out about no bins in the toilet cubicles.

I could tell she was cross with school. Mum says she's cross because that's a really basic thing – that the school should make sure there is somewhere to put used pads and Miss Peters should have thought about that. I begged her not to make a big fuss at school. She said we could go together tomorrow to the school office and ask them what to do. She said I'm a pioneer! She's really strange sometimes.

Then she started talking about what I'd like to do to mark my first period (my menarche apparently). She says she knows someone that had a period party! With a red cake!! There's no way I want that. Instead we, just mum and me, and not Dante (my brother), are going to go to the café and get a tuna sandwich. That's my favourite. (I do love baking though. Maybe we can make Red Velvet cupcakes as long as mum promises not to say they're anything to do with periods.)

12th February DAY 4

Today there was hardly any blood at all. I didn't have to change my pad all day at school.

Mum said I can write down how I feel all the way through the month. She showed me an app on her phone that looks cool because you can write down how you're feeling and you can add emojis. So I asked if I'm getting a phone then and she said "No way, you're too young." That does not make any sense! Why show me an app if I can't have a phone?! So it's just you and me Period Diary. My mum gave this diary to me the same day as the necklace. She said she only started tracking her cycle at 34 years old. Just think how many more diaries I'll have compared to her!

Mum said we can write down what day we are on, on the family calendar. In red pen! She says it's helpful for everyone in the family to know what day of our cycle we're on. But what if my friends come around and notice? Mum said it's like a code and only our family know what it's about.

I'm on Day 4 and my mum's on Day 27. She says that's why she's been a bit grumpy today. I didn't notice any difference to usual to be honest. I just read that sentence again - I don't mean she's always grumpy!! Haha.

13th February   DAY 5

I'm SO excited. Tomorrow Rose is coming to stay. She's as tall as my dad and has shoulder length brown hair and brown eyes. I have blue eyes, but people say we look alike otherwise. She's really kind.

We went to the café, just mum and me, for a celebration tuna sandwich. My brother Dante was at gym club after school. It was so nice because we don't usually have time just the two of us together. This was the best way to celebrate my first period for me, but I hope we can do this every time I have a period!!

14th February   DAY 6

Rose was at home when I got back from school. It was so nice to see her. When mum went to cook dinner, I told her my big news. She said "oh" and gave me a big hug. Rose said she was 16 when her periods started. And I'm 10! I guess everyone is different. She said her period is a right pain because she's super sporty and she doesn't run as fast when she has her period. I don't think I wanted to move at all last Saturday. I can't imagine running then!

I asked what athletes do who run in the Olympics or play tennis in Wimbledon if they have their period. She said sometimes they don't do as well, but scientists are beginning to see how they can help women athletes use their cycle, doing different kinds of training at different times of the month. It's amazing to think there are people in the world that study periods!

29th March DAY 1

My period came again. 44 days since the last one! Sorry I haven't written anything for a while Dear Diary but life went back to normal. I went into town and got a new denim jacket with a unicorn on it. I got three house points in one day at school. I had to go to the dentist. That's all that's happened since last time I wrote.

It was school today and my tummy was hurting so much after breakfast (except mum said it's not my tummy really but my womb). She said I could stay home if I wanted, but I didn't want to miss the class treat that was happening. She gave me a secret bar of chocolate in my bag in case I was feeling sad and told me to tell Miss Peters if I felt too bad.

It was ok actually. Being with my friends distracted me and I didn't use as many pads as last time. There is only a special bin for period pads in the teachers' toilet, so I have to go there. It's a bit of a pain because I have to remember to take my bag with me, with the pads in. Charlie in my class asked me why I was going home and I said I'm not. I didn't want to say what I WAS doing. I felt a bit embarrassed.

As soon as I got home I asked for a hot water bottle. Not because my tummy (I mean womb) was hurting any more but because I wanted to feel snuggly. Mum got me a blanket and tucked me up on the sofa. She got a tea and sat for ages stroking my head. It was really nice.

30th March DAY 2

One of the teachers, Mr Seston, asked me why I was using the teachers' toilet today and I said it was women's business since that's what my dad calls it. He looked cross and said please go back to the Year 5 toilets. I said that Miss Peters told me to use the teachers' toilet so I have somewhere to put my pads. The look on his face changed and he went bright RED! He mumbled something and went off very quickly! It was actually quite funny AFTER it happened. I couldn't wait to tell mum when I got home.

I was really tired after school today and watched TV

for a while (more than one hour). I watched Horrible Histories and it made me laugh loads. Usually I help put the forks and glasses out for dinner, but today I didn't feel like it and my mum said I didn't have to.

She laughed when I told the story about Mr Seston and said well done for standing my ground. I'm not sure what that means but I could tell she was very proud of me. Miss Peters has been really nice and said to go to the toilet whenever I need to. I discovered that we have a RED BOX at school so if I ever forget my stuff, I can get a pad from the office.

31st March DAY 3

We have swimming on Thursdays and I was a bit worried about the blood coming out in the pool. I love swimming so I really wanted to go. Mum said I could try a menstrual cup or a tampon (that you put inside to collect or soak up the blood). Someone in Year 6 who's in art club said that you can't use a tampon for the first year. But mum said you can if you feel ready. The cup looked big, even when you fold it to put it inside, so I decided I would try a tampon. Mum got one that said organic cotton on the box because otherwise the chemicals might irritate my skin or make my period heavier!

So I had a go. You have to take the plastic cover off and pull the little string down. I tried with the normal one, but couldn't seem to push it in. You have to get the right angle as you push it inside. Mum said she could come in and help me, but I wanted to try to do it myself.

I tried a few more times, then asked mum if she could show me how she would do it (with her clothes on!). She showed me a sort of squatting position and a picture of where you actually put it inside your body. That helped but then she found a tampon with an applicator (a bit of cardboard around it - my cousin lives near a beach in Wales and she said they find plastic applicators from tampons on the sand nearly every time they go so I'm happy this was a cardboard one). That was so much easier. I managed to put it in, and it felt a bit weird. I'm not sure it was in the right place, but I was so chuffed that I'd done it.

I was going to keep the tampon in, but then I realised I didn't know how to take it out! My mum said I'd better practice that. I pulled on the string but it felt really strange. I suddenly felt a bit scared – like I might not ever get it out.

Mum asked me to come and have breakfast and then I could have another go at taking it out as she talked me through it. She gave me a big hug. She said it's really important to relax when you pull on the string. And it's easier when the tampon is soaked in blood (I haven't left it in long enough yet for that to happen she thinks). After breakfast, I went into the bathroom again and she told me jokes through the door until I laughed. It was easier when I relaxed.

I decided I wasn't ready to do all this by myself. I was so sad if I was going to miss swimming, but mum said she'll take me at the weekend and we could practice using the tampons again so it gets easier. It's a bit hard, this period stuff, sometimes.

1st April DAY 4

Dad said he'd started his period. Mum and I didn't find it funny, even when he said it was only an April Fool's joke. Dante thought it was HILARIOUS though. Then it turned out that he didn't even know what a period was. Little brothers are really silly. My mum told him that a period is when a baby hasn't been made and special blood comes out. Dante jumped around the kitchen looking grossed out.

I WhatsApp'd Rose on my mum's phone and told her about Dante jumping around. She laughed. I also told her about the Mr Seston story too. I felt I was in a special club that girls go into when they start their period! Then we went back to talking about what we'd been watching on YouTube. She's so lucky – because she's a grown up now she can watch whatever she likes, but mum is always checking what I watch.

2nd April DAY 5

Beth B and I did the most amazing poster at school today. We got a house point each.

Beth's been my friend forever. We went to pre-school together. She's really good at English, whereas I'm better at maths. We help each other out.

I didn't have to change my pad all day. It was an easy day.

9th April

In my knickers today it looked wet, but I knew I hadn't done a wee in them! I asked mum and she said in the middle of the cycle you can sometimes see fluid and it's perfectly normal. She said it can be white, yellowish or like mine – transparent. I have had it a little bit before, but I thought it was wee to be honest. It made me think about how just before Christmas I saw a tiny bit of blood in my knickers (like one spot!!) and thought I'd started my period, but nothing else happened. Mum said it was a sign that it could start soon. Mum said this fluid in the middle of the cycle is called discharge or vaginal mucous, and it's a sign that you're healthy. I must admit I smelt it, but it didn't really smell of anything.

9th May

My period hasn't started yet, but I felt so daydreamy today. I couldn't concentrate in class and Miss Peters said my name three times before I realised she was talking to me. Oops!

10th May DAY 1

I woke up earlier than usual this morning and low in my womb ached a bit. I got out of bed to go to the toilet and saw blood in my PJs. I managed not to get it on the sheets. 42 days this time from my last period.

11th May DAY 2

My period was a bit heavier today compared to yesterday. Like last time, it was bit heavier on Day 2 than Day 1.

12th May DAY 3

I still prefer pads at the moment. Mum bought some reusable ones for me. They're really cute – one's got flamingos on, another has blue cats, another has palm trees and the last one has dolphins. I think they're good for the environment. My friend has a baby sister and she has reusable nappies. They make her look funny because her bottom looks big and padded. My pads aren't like that at all – they are slim and you can't see them through my clothes. Also I don't have to go to the teacher's toilet – I just put them in a waterproof bag and take them home. I'm not sure about using them on the second day when it's heavier. I'm still getting used to it all. I was worried it might smell to have them in my bag, but it doesn't.

13th May DAY 4

Sam in my class was in big trouble today. He said a rude word at the teacher and had to see the headteacher, Mr Clocker.

24th May

Today there was a bake sale at school. It was Year 5's turn and I made some chocolate brownies with strawberry jam in. Everyone said they were DELICIOUS. I had a big smile all the way walking home.

31st May

Maya in Year 6 looked sad today at breaktime. I know her from art club. We became friends even though we're in different years because we're taller than anyone else! I went over and sat with her. She started crying! I said, "What's the matter?" At first, she didn't want to say anything and then she whispered that she thinks she started her period. She hadn't told anyone but instead had stuffed toilet paper in her knickers. I didn't have any pads with me because I only just finished my period about a week ago.

I said, "Why don't we go to the school office and ask for pads?" She shook her head, but I said that I'd already gone to talk to them with my mum about bins to put the used pads in. Her eyes got wider, and she said, "Have you started then?". I said "Yes" and so she agreed to go as long as I asked!

Miss Fletcher in the office said well done for helping a friend. They had some spare pads in the office.

Wouldn't it be better if your teacher at the beginning of the year said she had spare pads if you needed them in the cupboard? In front of everyone. So you know where to go? Maybe I could write this and put it in the suggestions box in the school office. Mum's always putting suggestions in there. She's that kind of person!

24th May   DAY 15

I was full of energy today and was having fun playing rounders. Then one of the boys elbowed me in the chest by accident and it hurt SO much. The little bumps (breast buds my mum calls them) are so much bigger now and they're so ouchy when they're touched. I'm sure one is a bit bigger than the other, but my mum says that's normal. I don't know how my mum knows all this stuff!

I know it's Day 15 because I counted from my last period. My mum said that in the middle of the cycle you can feel like you have more energy. It's the hormones changing. I feel like I could run around the garden all afternoon! I love this feeling. My mum said to watch out because I won't have the same energy all month. Sometimes she feels like superwoman in the middle of the cycle, but she can say yes to too many things and then feel exhausted before her period.

25th May   DAY 16

Mum took me bra shopping today. In Year 5, we still have to change in the classroom with the boys for PE. In Year 6 the girls change first in the classroom and then the boys. I've been wearing a crop top for ages under my school dress but it's getting too hot now. The boys don't look, they're too busy messing around. It's the other girls! I think because I'm ahead of the others they are interested to see what breasts look like. It makes me feel shy.

When I was trying on bras at in the dressing room at the shop, I looked in the mirror and I was sure that one was a bit bigger than the other. The lady who was helping with the sizing overheard me telling my mum. It was totally AWKWARD! She said it's perfectly normal and not to worry. I couldn't look at her face when I went out again. I forgot the changing cubicle doesn't have solid walls.

22th June DAY 1

My period arrived. I counted back on the calendar and it was 44 days since the last one. How are you meant to know when it's going to come when it's different each time? My mum says be patient because my body is getting used to the hormones and the right levels for me. She says her period comes about every 30 days, but Rose said hers is 27 or 28 days. My auntie says hers is 26 days! It seems everyone's a bit different.

I heard mum talking to our next-door neighbour. She said that she's on the Pill and so her period comes exactly every 28 days and she couldn't put up with not knowing when it's coming. The pill sounds really good. I'll have to ask mum about it. I wonder why she doesn't use it?

23rd June DAY 2

Ouch! It was really hurting today. I even felt a bit dizzy. I stayed in the school office at lunchtime. It was too noisy in the playground. I felt like going home, but nobody asked me about phoning my mum. I was so relieved when mum picked me up at home time. As soon as we got on to our road, I burst into tears. Mum made me my favourite dinner – pasta and dough balls. She's the best.

Rose sent me a nice message. She sent me a selfie with tampons stuck up her nostrils! She's SO funny. Don't do that at home people!! I can't wait to see her in the school holidays.

24th June DAY 3

I asked my mum about the Pill and if I can go on it. She asked where I heard about it and I said I heard something on the radio. I didn't want her to know I'd been listening to her conversations!! She said she thought it was a bit early to think about it. The Pill is a 'contraceptive'. I didn't know what that is, but she explained it's to stop you getting pregnant.

I said I only wanted to make my periods come at the

same day each month. Mum said that some girls take the Pill for bad acne or heavy periods, but you have to be really careful because it can have side effects. Mum says each girl needs to think about what's right with her, with her mum or someone else who can help her make decisions. She said in the first few years that your body is getting used to the new amounts of hormones and if you take the Pill in that time, your body can get confused and not know how to control the hormones by itself.

I said is it a bit like being able to ride a bicycle yourself, without stabilisers helping you balance. She said not really, but sort of. Haha! Thanks mum SO helpful. Not knowing when my period will come doesn't seem so bad now.

25th June

There is a lot about having your period which is good in my house. My mum makes a fuss, a nice fuss. Like a bath with a bath bomb in. Or giving me a foot massage.

But I was wondering, if we ever have our periods at the same time, who will do that for me? No-one ever gives mum a foot massage. I've decided that next time she's on her period, I'm going to do something nice for her.

26th June DAY 5

I am so happy! Today was swimming at school and I used tampons! There wasn't much blood in the morning, but I didn't want to risk it coming out.

I feel like I can do anything now when I have my period! I might even try the menstrual cup soon.

2
Disaster strikes

25th July   DAY 1

The last day of school and disaster ☹ We were having the last assembly of the year and as usual Year 5 were sitting on the floor. My womb had hurt a bit earlier in the morning, but I didn't think anything about it because it's only been 35 days since my last period.

The assembly went on and on because there were special awards and because Year 6 were leaving (some of the girls were crying!). When we finally got up to go, Leah next to me screamed. Really high pitched and EVERYONE looked round. She pointed at my dress, actually pointed, and said "There's blood!" in a squeaky voice. I knew immediately what had happened but didn't know what to do. I didn't even have a jumper to put round my bottom.

Miss Peters came over to see why Leah had screamed. And I mouthed 'period' at her. I don't think she understood until I turned around. So she stood behind me and said to the others to file out as normal. Everyone looked at my face on the way out. I just looked at the floor. I think they thought that I'd done something bad to Leah.

On the last day ☹️☹️. I can't believe it. Miss Peters found a spare dress, but it didn't fit very well. I had pads in my bag. I always carry them now in a pencil case because I never know quite when my periods will start. I put the dress with the blood on in my waterproof bag to take home. Miss Peters was very kind and said it had happened to her too – when she was wearing WHITE trousers! But that was in a class of 30 children, not 200 in a hall!!!!!!!

When I got home, I got totally upset and said everyone will remember me as the period girl. Mum said she could see why I was upset, but most of them didn't know what had actually happened and would probably think I cut my leg if they did see the blood because very few had started their periods and the younger children probably didn't even know what one is. She said they'll forget all about it over the holidays, but I'm not so sure.

26th July DAY 2

So happy there is NO school today. I don't want to see any of my friends.

17th July DAY 3

Today I wore disposable pads because we were going to Legoland and I didn't want to carry the used reusable ones round all day. Suddenly I felt a sharp pain near my vulva and went "ow" out loud. Mum asked if I was alright and I said I had to go to the toilet. We had already been in the queue for the ride for half an hour and Dante really whined when mum said we had to leave the queue. I said I could go by myself, but I think mum was worried about me.

This is what a vulva looks like in the book my mum gave me...

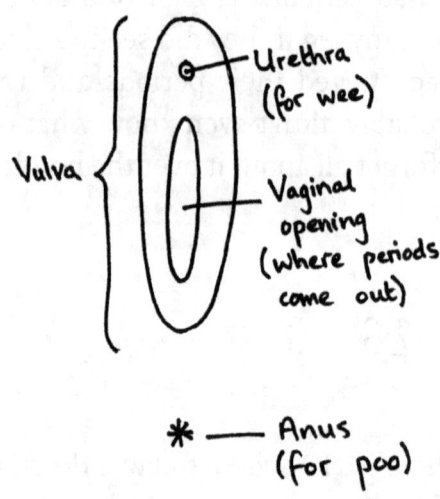

When I went to the toilet, I realised what had happened. The sticky bit of the pad had stuck on my pubic hair. I've only got 11 hairs down there! I counted!! And it had to get stuck on one of them. I put a new pad and made sure the wings were wrapped around my knickers properly.

Mum asked me if I was ok when I came out and I just gave her a rude stare. I feel bad now, but I feel really fed up of having periods when I'm only 10. Why do I have to put up with this when all the other 10-year-old girls at Legoland are just excited about the next ride or what they're having for lunch. Grrrrrrrrrrrrrrrrrrrrrrrr.

28th July DAY 4

I had a lazy day today and I feel a lot better. I read my favourite book of the moment The World's Worst Teachers, which made me laugh a lot. I also watched five episodes of my favourite thing on YouTube, Mr Kate. I want to be an interior designer when I grow up. I've planned my whole bedroom for when I'm allowed to change it. I'm going to have one wall a sort of Rose Pink colour and the others neutral. I want to have soft cushions and some fairy lights along my shelves. I even tried drawing it, but it was quite tricky to get everything in the right place.

I think yesterday I should have had a lazy day. Legoland was just too busy while I was having my period. I did cope, but I didn't have as much fun as normal. That's ok I guess.

29th July DAY 5

Beth B came over for a play date. She didn't even mention the disaster. Even when I hinted a bit about the assembly. Maybe mum is right – people won't remember. Or care!

30th July DAY 6

Today I got some blood on my knickers. Usually my period is finished by Day 5 so I didn't put a pad in. It was a bit brown instead of red. Not much, but it surprised me. Mum washed my knickers in cold water with some soap so the blood wouldn't stain. She hung them up in the bathroom to dry! I didn't want Dante to think I'd wet myself so I put them on the handle of the back of my door instead.

1st September

Pinch, punch, first of the month and no returns!

I woke up to find spots all over my chin. I've had one or two before, but not this many. They're huge. And just before school is starting back. I was looking through the cupboards for something to put on them, but Rose (she's been staying the last 10 days 😊) said it's better not to put on anything too strong. She says she used to use Aknedoron, which is made of natural things. It sounds like an alien, but must be good because she has really clear skin now.

I heard toothpaste is good for putting on spots. Rose says maybe not such a good idea, and try not to pick them! Dad showed me videos on YouTube of people picking their spots! Totally GROSS. How did he know they existed? There are strange people out there.

2nd September

Still spotty. I went shopping with mum today for new school uniform and she says I've shot up! I'm now in 11-12 sizes even though I'm 10. She said that it's all the manure she puts in my boots. She's always said that.

The main problem is that the white shirts that should be for my age don't fit very well round my boobs. (My mum calls them breasts, but that always sounds weird to me.) I'm a head taller than the other girls in my class. Sarah in the other class is the same height as me. She's curvier too, but I don't know if she got her period. We don't really play in the same group, so I don't talk to her much. It would be nice if another girl in Year 5 had her period too though.

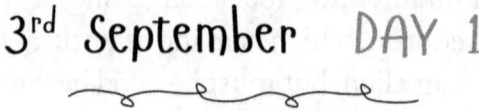

3rd September DAY 1

Period started. Mums says that explains the spots.

5th September DAY 3

First day back at school and I'm in Year 6. I can't believe I'm in the last year of primary. I'm super excited to be moving to big school, but I'm also excited to be the biggest in the school now. I've been in the same school since Foundation. I remember being a small kid there. It was lots of playing. That was the best year!

We've got Miss Peony now. She's really nice.

6th September DAY 5

I had swimming lessons after school today. Because there might be some blood, I used a tampon. But when I took it out afterwards it didn't feel very good. I asked my mum and she said that maybe because there wasn't much blood left, the material the tampon is made from was dragging on my inside skin. She said it can also irritate the skin inside because it soaks up anything, not just blood.

I was so confused. I thought nothing else comes out of the middle hole, because the wee comes out of the front hole. She said the vagina also has secretions (a kind of liquid) to keep it clean, like a self-cleaning oven! My mum says really strange things sometimes.

She also said that in the middle of the month you can get vaginal mucous. Remember how I found it my knickers before? Vaginal mucous sounds like snot that comes out of your vagina! Gross. But she said it's not gross but really useful and normal.

It can be see-through or white or even a bit yellow, and is stretchy like an elastic band. Or really wet in your pants. I said HOW is it useful? She didn't say anything for a minute and then took a deep breath and said that it can help semen travel up to the egg to make a baby. Yeah REALLY USEFUL mum! And still GROSS.

She said you can use a panty liner on those days, but it washes off no problem. Apparently you can get reusable panty liners too – they might be good for the last day of my period when hardly any blood is coming out.

7th September DAY 6

We have our trip away next week. Four nights away! I had a sleepover at Beth One's house once. And one at Katy's house for her 10th birthday, but I've never been away for four nights. I'm a bit glad that I already had my period.

12th September

(I'm writing this when I got back from the trip because I forgot to take you dear diary.) Emily got her first period on the trip. She was actually in my room (there were four girls). She woke up in the morning just like I did when I got my first period and the blood had come. I had been awake for about 10 minutes and was reading – it was a bit hard because there wasn't lots of light, but I didn't want to wake the others because it was before the alarm.

She woke up and yawned so I looked at her. Then she looked confused. She sat up in bed looking more confused. I pretended not to be looking, to give her some privacy, but I could hear she was pulling the duvet back. Then she gasped. I turned over in bed and could see the blood. I gave her a small smile and said "Congratulations!".

She looked even more confused. I whispered, "You got your period!" Her lower lip looked wobbly, so I got out of bed and asked if she wanted a hug? I said "I already got my period. I've had six already". She started to cry and that made me feel really bad – like I'd done something wrong, but I think she just totally wasn't expecting her period to start.

I asked her if she had any pads and she whispered "No". So I got my bag out. After last week I decided to take them everywhere. I gave her one of the disposable ones (I thought she'd be grossed out if she knew I'd already used the reusable ones even though they're cuter). I said we could tell the teacher and she would know where to get more.

She was worried about the sheet and being told off, but I said "It's nature and nobody's fault". I don't know where that came from! It seemed to do the trick though because she got out of bed, found new knickers in her suitcase and went to the bathroom to change them. I said "My mum washes them with cold water and soap", but she just put them in a bag because there was only one day left of the trip.

She wanted me to go with her to see Miss Peony. The teacher was really nice. She didn't say congratulations but said she would ask where to get more pads and came back in 10 minutes with loads! They could have lasted three periods. Emily said thanks to me when we were alone later, and my heart felt like it would burst. Sometimes, just sometimes, it's nice being the one who's already started her periods!

14th September

Mum showed me some period pants that she bought for me. There were three pairs that came in a pack: turquoise, pink and yellow. I love turquoise. She said she didn't get them before because she wanted me to feel confident using other products. They seem just like normal knickers but a bit more crinkly when you scrunch the material. No more sticky strips sticking to your leg or pubes (that's pubic hair BTW)! I'm so excited for my next period so I can try them.

I wonder what girls do when their mums don't talk to them about this stuff?!

7th October   DAY 2

No leaking all night. The period pants are really good. I wore my third pair, but I didn't make it all day this time. I started to feel like I wanted to change them at lunchtime. Maybe because it's a heavier flow of blood on my second day. Luckily, I had a spare pair of normal knickers and pads with me. I'm always prepared now! For me and the other girls.

8th October   DAY 3

My mum found a pin badge with a single drop of blood on and a winking face. It might sound weird, but she's really cute. I asked if we could get one for Emily and Maya in the other class. When we get the badges, I'm going to say we can be a club now and maybe we can wear the badge on our coat if we have our period so we can look out for each other.

This is what my badge looks like, but with the drop coloured in red:

I've nicknamed her.... **Miss Drop**

9th October DAY 4

Beth B says that she's going to a Mother and Daughter workshop on Sunday. It sounds really cool. She's not sure what's going to happen except that they're talking about periods. I think because she knows I have my period she's excited rather than scared or nervous. She asked me what it feels like and I said that sometimes it's a bit achy on the first day, but ok really.

14th October

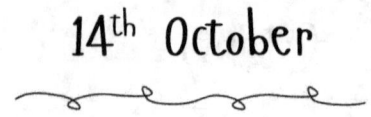

Beth B says it was really cool at the Mother and Daughter workshop and she wants to go again next Sunday! They talked about cycles and looked at all the period products. I said that I use period pants, tampons and pads, and Beth's eyes got all wide like she was impressed. She said there was also a cup, but I said I haven't tried that. My mum uses it, but it was hard enough getting the tampon in! I do want to try it at some point though. Beth said they have different colour cups too.

I told my mum about the Mother and Daughter thing and she said she would see if there's one for girls who've already started their periods.

15th October

It's my birthday on the 31st October. Halloween!! It's great having your birthday on Halloween because you always have lots of sweets and lots of fun dressing up even if your birthday is on a school day.

I've asked mum if I can have a spa party. We're going to have face masks, foot spas and a movie. I'm having four friends over: Beth B, Beth F, Emily and Celine who is French and new to our class, and really nice. They're going to sleep over and I said don't forget to bring your pads in case your period starts. They all rolled their eyes and we all started laughing. Beth B says she's going to get a pencil case like mine with spare knickers, pads and tissues so she's ready. Her mum's going to let her choose the pencil case.

31st October

My birthday. I am 11! Dad said "My Big Girl" in a really embarrassing way.

3rd November

My sleepover was yesterday and I was too busy to write. We all had lots of sweets from Halloween so we had the best midnight feast ever, and it was literally at midnight! We watched the Emojii movie. I missed it when it came out. Beth B and Emily had already watched it but said they didn't mind watching it again because it's really good. After the movie we talked about stuff. About how sometimes at school the other girls can makes comments about how you look. It felt really nice to talk together.

My mum goes to a Red Tent. When I was little I thought she went camping in an actual red tent, but really it's a group of women and they talk about their feelings. I know lots of the ladies because they're mum's friends and we meet up sometimes at the park or at each other's houses. I've known some of them since I was little, maybe four years old. They're like aunties. I think they talk about periods sometimes. I'm going to ask my mum if I can come to the Red Tent now I have my period. I think Red Tents are all over England, maybe the world.

Maybe they should make Pink Tents for girls!

6th November

Grrrrrrrrrrrrrrrrrrrr! I'm so fed up of my brother. He is REALLY annoying ☹ He's always coming up behind me wanting to see what I'm doing. He always wants to watch what I watch.

3
What's your favourite season?

8th November   DAY 1

Happy Day 1 to me!

9th November   DAY 2

My dad said maybe the reason I was so cross with Dante a few days ago was because I was coming up to my period. I don't even remember being cross with him, but it must be true because it's in my diary.

I guess I wasn't really cross at him, but just wanted to be a bit quiet and he kept chatting. Mum said it's nearly a year since I had my first period and maybe I could start keeping track of my cycle – all the way through the month and not just when I have my period. I said it's already on the calendar in red ink – her idea not mine ha ha - but she said writing down how I'm feeling, if I've got spots and stuff because there might be a pattern.

Mum's given me a sheet with different feelings on and space to add your own words (You can get one at www.cyclicalwisdom.com/rubylunachart. I'm going to give it a try.

10th November   DAY 3

	Day 1	Day 2	Day 3	Day 4	Day 5	Day 6	Day 7	Day 8	Day 9
Period	X	X	X						
Tired	X	X	X						
Cross									
Sad									
Happy									
Achy		X	X						
Spotty									
Energetic									
Chocolate		XXX							

I might use colour on my chart. Guess what red will be for? That's right, when I have my period. Today I ticked tired and achy.

12th November   DAY 5

No more blood. Mum calls this time after the period her Inner Spring. I still feel a bit tired, but good.

19th November   DAY 14

I have so much energy today. We were doing obstacle races at school today and I was really fast. I could have done the race again straight away. I might colour this yellow on the chart because yellow is the colour of the sun and the sun has lots of energy. Plants use photosynthesis with the sun to make energy. We've been doing that at school

I like the chart because I know exactly what day I am. Don't worry dear diary, I will still write in you. xx

30th November   DAY 25

Purple for being cross today. I felt really cross with Beth B today. She was talking about me with Kitty. She pretended she wasn't, but I could hear her. She's so annoying sometimes.

Mum was annoying me too. She said maybe I feel out of sorts because I'm coming up to my period. It's NOT because of that. I told her maybe she's annoying because of HER period. I went up to my room to be alone and slammed the door. I pressed so hard with the purple on my chart that it's gone through the paper a bit.

4th December DAY 29

See mum was wrong. I still haven't had my period. You can't blame everything on my period!

I'm really excited though because she said she's booked us on to a Celebration Day for Girls. I've never heard of it before, but it's for girls who are 10 to 12 years old and it's about cycles and stuff. I feel a bit nervous because there will probably be older girls there who know more. But I do have my period. Will all the girls have their period?

13th December DAY 1

37 days this time. Why does my period come when I'm wearing white knickers? How does it know? I'm happy that it's Saturday tomorrow when it's my heavier flow

day. Planning to lie around and do my homework on Sunday. Oh no! I can't – we're at the Celebration Day all day. Maybe mum will let me off doing my homework!

I just asked, and she said "Well done for thinking about it, you can do it now! You still have to do your homework young lady". I'm only a young lady when she's saying something like that!

14th December

I'm going to wear the necklace my mum gave me when I started my period. I feel excited and nervous at the same time about the workshop. Normally it's hard to talk to other girls at school about periods so I'm happy I can hear more about how they find it, but I feel nervous because I don't know who the teacher will be and what she'll be like.

I told the other Beth (Beth F) about the celebration day and she said it sounded boring and weird to talk about periods with a stranger all day. She said her mum left a book on her big sister's bed when her period started. Beth said she took it out of her sister's drawer to look at it, but she didn't look at it in the end because she won't get her period for ages. How does she know?

16th December DAY 4

(I'm writing this the day after the Celebration Day because I was so tired after). It was brilliant. The teacher was called Billy and she was really nice. She started her period at nine! One year earlier than me and she talked about how that made her feel. We did so much cool stuff. In the morning it was just us girls and Billy, then our mums came back in the afternoon. One girl looked like she really didn't want to be there and was very quiet when she spoke, but when her mum came back at lunchtime, she was talking at a thousand miles an hour about all the things she'd learnt.

Only one other girl had already started her period and she was 12 and had started at secondary school. There were two others who were 10, four who were 11, and two who were 12. They were from different schools, primary and secondary schools, but they were all really nice.

Some asked loads of questions and some were shy. I was in the middle. Before I went to the workshop, I didn't know whether I would say if I had my period, but one girl was asking if periods hurt and so I just started talking about how I felt on the first day of my periods. They all looked surprised because I was one of the younger ones.

We learnt lots of new stuff and Billy talked about tracking your cycle so I'm going to have another go at it. I sort of did it for a while and then forgot about it. The mums came back in the afternoon and there was a story and we made something with our mums and most of the mums got all teary. In the car on the way home, mum said it's because she can see I'm growing up, but she remembers when I was a little baby and the time has gone so fast. Something soppy like that!

It was really cool spending the afternoon with my mum. Dante went off to practise riding his bike without stabilisers with dad round the park. I wonder if they have Celebration Days for Boys?

PS. We put tampons in a jar of water and they swelled up so big! It was really fun seeing them like that. All the girls laughed.

17th December DAY 5

I WhatsApp'd Rose on mum's phone and told her about the Celebration Day. I asked if she went to one, but she said she didn't think they existed when she was my age. At least, not where she lived. She said she wishes she went to one as it sounded really good.

You I know I said she's sporty? She's doing a triathlon soon – you have to run, swim and ride a bicycle in a race! She says she would wear a menstrual cup if she had her period so she wouldn't need to change it during the race. But GUESS what? She said a lady – Kiran somebody – ran a marathon and didn't wear anything for her period because it was uncomfortable. I said but didn't the blood go everywhere? Rose said that it did show on her leggings, but Kiran didn't care.

Rose also said that athletes sometimes just wee when they're running!!! They don't stop and go to a toilet because they'd lose time so they just wee as they're running along! I don't see that's any different from your period leaking down your leg. Rose said it's because there's a taboo around menstruation (that's the posh word for period by the way). I don't know what a taboo is, but I didn't want to tell her that.

18th December DAY 6

Nearly finished for Xmas hols. So happy.

19th December DAY 7

Andreia from the Celebration Day sent a message through her mum to my mum because she wants to stay in touch. She was the other one who already had her period. She said on Sunday that no-one really talks about it in her class. She only knows if someone has her period because you can see them trying to hide a pad or tampon in their hand on the way to the toilet. I said "Yes, let's keep in touch". Mum says we can go out for a tuna sandwich all together!

I'm putting green on my chart because I feel different to when I have my period. More excited, more energy. I even want to play with my brother! Or maybe that's just because it's nearly Christmas ha ha.

20th December DAY 8

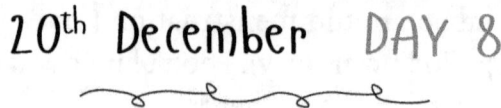

I feel really bad for Maya. She's the other one in Year 6 who has her period. I saw her at the school office yesterday when I took the register back. She was bent over and was holding her tummy and looked white. I asked what was wrong. She looked from side to side to see if anyone was listening and said her period had started and it was hurting so much. She said she bleeds so much and it was always leaking. It sounded so hard. I said maybe she could go home and get a hot water bottle, but she said no her mum told the school office to give her tablets to help with the pain. Her mum said to her "You just have to get on with it".

I wanted to stay with her, like my mum stays with me

if my womb's hurting, but Mrs Talbot in the office said I had to go back to class. She's really nice though and said she has a secret hot water bottle she uses at work when she has period cramps and winked as she went off to fill it with hot water! I've never seen her wink before.

I told my mum about Maya and Mrs Talbot and asked why her hot water bottle was secret and why she winked? Mum said it was because of the taboo around periods. That taboo again! She said that in our society periods are something that most people don't talk about openly, even though half the population will have them at some point. For some reason periods are often talked about as something to hide, or even that they are dirty, rather than something natural that means that babies can be born and humans can continue on planet earth.

I now see that my mum is NOT like most people. She LIKES talking about periods!

December 21st DAY 9

The Christmas holidays. Yay!! No more school for two weeks.

I decided I'm going to buy my mum a Christmas present. I don't get pocket money yet, but I asked dad if I could have some money. I'm going to buy her a special pen to write on her period chart. I saw a sparkly silver one that I think she will love.

I'm going to bake some biscuits for dad and decorate them: gingerbread reindeer with red icing on their noses. Dante only wants lego stuff. I asked for some big headphones so I hope I get them. I also asked for some money for playing my favourite computer game. It's where you can build your own house or café. I usually start with making a café because then I can make money in the game to buy more decorations for the house. I'm really good at decorating the houses. My friend Celine plays too and she asks me to decorate her house for her because I'm quicker at doing it.

December 22nd DAY 10

Still colouring my chart green. Mum says I'm a bit too full of energy. She gave me this today since I'm interested in charting again.

Inner Winter - Menstruation - Days 1-7

Inner Spring - Pre-ovulation - Days 8-14

Inner Summer - Ovulatory phase - Days 15-22

Inner Autumn - Pre-menstrum - Days 23-28.

It's definitely easier to talk about seasons than use those other words like ovulatory!

She said it's just a guide because women have different length cycles. Like me! Ovulation is when the egg pops out of the ovary. Mum said that girls often don't have ovulation for a few years after starting their period. I didn't know what Pre-Menstrum was but when she said, "What about PMS?" I had heard of that. The S is for Stress. We were joking around saying it could be PMI – I is for impatient, or PMC – C is for cross, or PMT – T is for tired (although she said PMT already is used for Pre-Menstrual Tension).

Mum's friend Anna was around so they started talking about how they try to rest through the cycle, and to have a little bit of alone time around the Inner Autumn so they didn't feel stressed then. Anna said she locks herself in the bathroom for five minutes so she can get some peace and quiet!!

23rd December   DAY 11

Mum's busy cooking ready for Christmas day so I'm reading my diary. I like the idea of the seasons because in Summer you are full of energy to play outside, whereas in Winter you want to be cosy and inside more. In Spring the energy is more, just like flowers sticking their head out of the ground or animals waking up after hibernation. I'm not sure about Autumn because that's a time of harvest normally. But with the cycle it seems to be a time of wanting to be alone or you get annoyed with people. Maybe as it starts to get colder you want to be inside more doing your own thing rather than going on holiday with others?

I am in my Inner Spring right now, but that feels weird when we've just started real Winter outside. Mum said that when it's the same season inside and out you can feel stronger emotions. She said when it's her period, so her Inner Winter AND it's outer Winter, she feels like she needs to hibernate like a bear in a cave, "all by herself, alone, on her own" (to quote Lola from Charlie and Lola). If it's her Inner Winter but it's outer Summer, she's happy lying on the grass resting with kids playing nearby.

24th December   DAY 12

Christmas Eve and I can't sleep. Too excited

27th December   DAY 14

I totally forgot to write the last two days. For Christmas I got the headphones and the money for the computer game, but I also got a Moon Calendar diary. I think my mum is definitely behind the moon stuff! She has this really cool poster in her bedroom that shows how the moon is every day. It's dark blue with silver moons and it looks a bit like a wave. She once laid out the posters from the last five years and it make such a beautiful pattern from New Moon to Full Moon and back again.

I looked outside but the moon is completely hidden by the clouds right now.

Yesterday was Boxing Day and lots of family came around for the day. More presents ☺ I got this book from my Aunt called Create This Book and you have to colour it in and do the drawing challenges. Rose got me a different book called Wreck This Journal and you have to destroy it! You can rip it up and spill stuff on it.

I was so full of energy today that I did about HALF the Create This Book!!!!

And I washed up the plates and mum nearly fell off her chair in shock.

28th December DAY 15

I'm might be in my Inner Summer now but I don't really feel any different. I did notice that my knickers were a bit wet – I guess it's that discharge that mum told me about.

29th December   DAY 16

I went round to Celine's house today because they didn't go to France to see their family and so she invited me over. I met her older brother for the first time. He's called Jean (but he prefers JP short for Jean Paul) and he's 15. I wouldn't tell anybody else Dear Period Diary but I got butterflies in my tummy whenever he talked to me. Normally I'm quite a confident person but when he talked to me I couldn't say anything (he asked me to pass the bread and where my older sister lives in Italy). I just mumbled.

30th December   DAY 17

I didn't have anything else to do so I joined mum and did some yoga. She uses a video on YouTube. It was very nice actually. At the end I laid with my head on mum's tummy and we chilled out. Until we got the giggles and my head was bouncing up and down as she laughed. Dante came in and wanted to join in, but he ended up standing on my hair.

31st December   DAY 18

It's New Year's Eve tonight and we're going to have a party at home with my grandma and grandpa. We're all dressing up and I'm helping mum make mocktails – cocktails that are ok for children to drink because there's no alcohol. Mum said she'd got a surprise for us.

1st January   DAY 19
(or Day 1 of the New Year!!)

Happy New Year dear diary! It was really fun last night. The best thing was that the surprise is that we are going to get a kitten. Mum says we can pick up the kitten in about four weeks. I asked what colour the kitten will be and mum says the mummy cat is black, but who knows what colour our kitten will be?! I know I said I wanted a pug dog, but a kitten is just as good.

We've got to get everything ready, so tomorrow we're going to go and get a bed, bowl and scratching post. We were talking about names, but dad said let's wait until we meet the kitten.

2nd January   DAY 20

I woke up feeling really grumpy this morning. Even though we had so much fun last night and even though we're getting a kitten. And I've wanted a pet for forever. Dad said I was quiet at breakfast.

Mum said maybe it's where I am in my cycle – Day 20 and I'm probably in my Inner Autumn. She said when she was a bit older than me, she would go for a long walk listening to music on her Walkman (what they used before you could play music on a phone!). She would think "What's wrong with me? Why do I feel like this?" and now she realises it was just where she was in her cycle – it was always in her Inner Autumn that she felt like this. She wishes she had had a map of the Inner Seasons when she was a tween so she didn't spend so much time worrying about how she felt.

Grandma suggested going for a walk would help. If it had been mum or dad suggesting a walk I would have said "No way!", but I didn't want to be grumpy with grandma. While we were walking to the park, I asked grandma how her periods are. She looked surprised and said that she hasn't had periods for years because she's gone through the menopause. I never heard of that before! She said it's as the word says a pause of the monthly cycle. 'Mens' means month in Latin.

She said once you've not had a period for one year you are officially postmenopausal. Then you never have a period again. She said some of her friends are happy to not have a period anymore, but she sometimes misses it. When she first started her period, they had a thing with a belt around the waist and then straps that hung down and held the pad in place. She said it would always move around and would often leak. In some countries, girls still don't have good menstrual products to use and so have to use dirty rags or just miss school. That seems really unfair.

It was a cold day so we didn't stay in the park long but we went past the shop and grandma treated me to a magazine called Kookie. It's brilliant! Although I started the day grumpy, I was so glad I talked to my grandma as I felt much better afterwards.

3rd January   DAY 21

Grandma showed me how to make profiteroles today. They were deeeelicious.

4th January   DAY 22

Grandma and grandpa went home today and I felt sad

because they don't live that close. They promised to come back soon to visit when the kitten arrived.

5th January   DAY 23

I noticed today that my pubic hair is getting longer and darker. Maybe a bit curly as well! I kind of like it and kind of think it's strange. It doesn't feel like the hair on my head! Would it be weird to brush it?

6th January   DAY 24

Back to school today and I felt tired. Mum said the next two terms will go so quickly and then I'll have finished primary school forever. We don't find out which school I'm going to until March though. I get butterflies in my tummy when I think about it.

4
Butterflies in the heart

7th January   DAY 25

Charlie smiled at me today. I never noticed before, but he's got nice eyes. He's one of the clever boys in class and doesn't mess around. I remember he came second in Sport's Day last year because he and Sohail were running at the same speed and at the last minute Sohail stuck his head out and won! One of the Foundation boys was so cute because he didn't know you had to run in a straight line and so he ran across the lanes to his mum as fast as he could instead of to the finishing line!!

8th January   DAY 26

Grr. Everything went wrong today. My water bottle

leaked in my bag and made all the books wet. I don't know why it was upside down. My pencil case opened upside down and everything went everywhere all over the floor. Miss Peony told me off for talking, but I didn't know the lesson had started. She said "Ruby Luna, you are very distracted today!" Charlie looked at me and I went bright red. SOOOO embarrassing.

Rose rang mum in the evening to arrange when she's going to visit for half term holidays and I spoke to her for a while. I said what a horrible day I'd had. She said she finds it really hard to park the car when she's coming up to her period. Normally she's brilliant at parking because she lives in Trieste in Italy where the streets are narrow and you have to be super quick at parking because otherwise drivers beep their horn at you. But when it's the last few days before her period she suddenly can't get the angles right! She said maybe I was being clumsy because of that and not to feel bad about it.

Mum came into the room and said she gets really sensitive to noise close to her period. If everyone's talking and the radio is on it's just too much. She said her friend always dreams about her mum just the night before her period starts! I guess everybody is different. I hope I'm not clumsy tomorrow.

I know I'm really sensitive about how my friends feel. I can tell if someone's sad before anyone else notices. Mum said I could be a Highly Sensitive Person. I thought that sounded like a bad thing, but she said it means you might have more empathy than other people and be more affected by your surroundings. There's a documentary about it that she said we can watch next time I'm on my period.

9th January DAY 27

It was Dante's birthday today so he had his party at a trampolining place. Mum said I could invite one friend to keep me company so I asked Beth One. At the last minute she couldn't come and I was so upset. Her mum said she wasn't feeling well, but she was fine yesterday. Mum said we could see if Beth Two was free and luckily she was. Beth Two does gymnastics and she was so good on the trampoline.

I helped mum make Dante's cake. He wanted a pirate ship, but that was too difficult, so we make a treasure chest instead. It had gold chocolate coins inside and crushed up digestive biscuits for the sand outside. It was really good. Dante loved it and didn't want to cut it up.

10th January   DAY 28

I felt ok yesterday but today I feel tired and grumpy. Dad calls it feeling 'out of sorts'. It's probably the cycle again, but it's really annoying. I want to feel like I do in my Inner Summer – FULL of energy and happy happy happy - all the time.

11th January   DAY 29

I was getting changed at swimming class after school next to Sally who's in the first year of secondary school and she dropped her knickers on the floor. There was a bit of brown in them, but at the front (not at the back where poo would be). She looked embarrassed and picked them up quickly because she could see I'd been looking. I got on with getting changed and she suddenly said "It might be my period, it's not poo you know!" Now I felt embarrassed. I said "It's ok, I've started my period".

She said "Well I thought I had, but that was ages ago – before the summer holidays. But it was brown and not red. It's just been spots on my knickers – I thought there'd be loads of blood. My mum says there can be big gaps in between when you start your periods.

Maybe I'll get a proper one this time." I said "It's good to carry pads with you all the time now" and I told her how I never know when my next one is coming. It could be tomorrow, it could be weeks.

12th January   DAY 30

😊 😊 😊 Charlie handed me a note today and said to read it later. I was really confused but when I opened the note it said "It's nearly Valentine's Day. Will you come to the cinema with me?" I got big butterflies in my tummy.

I haven't shown it to anyone yet.

13th January   DAY 31

I had to show mum this morning because I needed to work out what I would say to Charlie. I felt really embarrassed when I handed her the note. I am embarrassed a lot at the moment!!!

She read it and her eyes got bigger like she was surprised. She said "Do you like this Charlie then?" and I had to squeak "Yes". Mum asked "Do you want to go to the cinema with him?" Another squeak "Yes!" "What will you see?" "I don't know mum". "How will you get there?" "I don't know." So many questions! She said "How exciting! I'll speak to his mum about who will drive you to the cinema. I hope it's my mum – it would be SOOO embarrassing to have to go in the car with his mum.

I saw Charlie in the playground before school but he was with his friends and didn't look over. At lunchtime he came and stood near me and my friends. I looked over and nodded yes. Beth and Catherine noticed and said "What's all that about?" and started teasing me (in a nice way). I didn't tell them yet!

14th January   DAY 32

My boobs felt a bit lumpy today. Sort of ouchy and uncomfortable. As soon as I got home I went upstairs and took my bra off.

15th January   DAY 1

Inner Winter at last. And it's Winter outside too.

I went swimming with Beth Two today after school. I used a tampon for going swimming. When we got back to Beth's house I needed to change it because it had started to feel a bit heavy. Then I realised I didn't know where to put it! There was no bin in her downstairs toilet and I thought I can't walk through the kitchen to put it in the bin there. So I had to put it in my waterproof bag where I put my reusable pads.

When I told mum about it when I got home she said I did really well. She said that made her think that we could have a little bin in our toilet at home and some pads and things for girls to use. A period-friendly house!!

16th January DAY 2

Mum talked with Charlie's mum in the playground today. I could see them through the classroom window before we finished. It felt very weird knowing they were talking about us going to the cinema.

After I got home, we watched the documentary 'Sensitive – The Untold Story'. It was really good – I felt the same as some of the people who talked in the film who said they are highly sensitive to how other people are feeling or what's happening around them. It made me feel that it's not so different to be sensitive or need some time to hang out in my room. Mum said it's good to know what we need to feel well and happy, but you've also got to tell other people what you need.

You can't expect them to know. It's not always obvious.

17th January   DAY 3

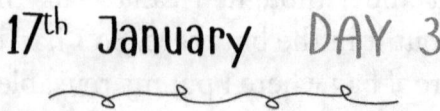

I was daydreaming today. What should I wear to the cinema? My mum's going to take us and Charlie's mum is going to pick us up. They decided we'd each buy our own ticket. I'm going to make some special popcorn with butterscotch on it to take to the cinema. Mum made some over Christmas and it was yummy.

18th January   DAY 4

Today I was using the teacher's toilet to change my pads. I'd run out of reusable ones and period pants and had to use some disposable pads instead. The headteacher saw me coming out and asked what I was doing. So I said what I'd said to Mr Seston: "It's women's business". Mr Croakley got it straight away though and nodded "Well that's ok then".

When I got home I said to mum, "Why did I have to get my period when I was only 10?!" Mum said she'd been reading about why girls are getting periods earlier than they used to. In the Victorian times, girls usually got their period between 16 and 17 years old because they had such poor diets! The food they ate wasn't very good and that meant it took longer for them to start getting their periods.

But then she said that girls in Ancient Rome (400AD) started at 13 or 14 years old. So I was thinking: did the girls in Ancient Rome have better food than the Victoria girls? Mum said it must be the excellent food she cooks that meant I started at 10. She was only joking, I think.

She said there are more hormones in the environment now – from how animals are farmed and that all gets into our food and our water. She said it can run in families too, if your mum got her period early then the daughter might too, but my mum got her period at 12.

19th January   DAY 5

23rd January   DAY 9

I went with Beth Two and her mum to the shop today on the way back to her house. Her mum, Kailash, sent us off to get bananas but when I came back she was putting pads into her shopping basket, under other stuff. Then when we went to the check out, she sent us off to wait outside. It's like she didn't want us, or me, to see the pads.

My dad buys tampons for me sometimes. He says sometimes he gets women smiling at him and other times they give him a weird look. Like he shouldn't be in that aisle. He said the first time he ever had to buy tampons for his sister he wasn't sure what size to get, and a woman spent ages going through the options with him. She said she was a nurse.

He also said that tampons are really good for starting fires when you go camping. You take off the plastic and fluff the cotton out. Then you can light it with a match. I don't know how he found THAT out!

25th January   DAY 11

I practiced making the butterscotch popcorn and it was really good.

I told Beth One and Beth Two about going to the cinema with Charlie and they were really giggly. They kept smiling at Charlie during maths and PE, and I had to tell them to stop.

27th January DAY 13

I started a diving course today. There were four boys and three girls. We were practising from the lower boards. The boards move quite a lot as you walk to the end and you have to breathe deeply and be still as you prepare to dive. We started with kneeling, then standing. At the end the teacher said to us "Do you want to go off the top board?" The top board is solid, but really high up. I didn't want to, but then the boys said yes and started going up the steps. I thought I'm going to do it if the boys are going to.

When I got to the top, I looked for my mum in the viewers' gallery and waved. She gave me a thumb's up, so I went to the edge and looked down. It was a long way! Two boys had already gone off (the other two weren't looking so sure now). I took a deep breath and dived off before I thought about it anymore. I felt AMAZING when I swam up to the surface.

When I saw mum after getting changed into dry clothes she said was really impressed.

2nd February

We went to get the kitten today! He's all black with yellowy, greeny eyes and is very sweet.

We took him home in his cat box and put him on the kitchen floor. He immediately weed everywhere. He looked a little bit scared and ran behind the washing machine. When mum tempted him out with some cat biscuits he was very dusty, so we call him Dusty. "Very original" said my dad. He was being sarcastic.

13th February

Sorry I've not written for a while dear Diary. I've been busy with Dusty. He's finding his way around the house and he's got a favourite spot on my pillow!

Tomorrow is the trip to the cinema with Charlie. I made the popcorn and put it in a bag, tied with a ribbon. It looks really good. I've got my clothes out that I'm going to wear. I've got butterflies.

14th February

Happy Valentine's! NOT! We went to the cinema and we bought our tickets. We sat down ready to watch the film and while we were watching the adverts, I gave Charlie the popcorn. He said "Thanks, I love popcorn". He took the ribbon off and we both had a handful. Then when he put his hand in again to get more, the whole bag tipped over and went all over the floor! I know it was an accident, but he just said "Oh well" and sat back like it didn't matter. I practised making the popcorn and put lots of effort into making it look nice and all he said was "Oh well".

The film was really good, but I just felt super annoyed after that.

Mum asked me how it went and I just crossed my arms and didn't want to talk about it. I went and stroked Dusty because he wouldn't ask any questions.

5
Endings & Beginnings

22nd February DAY 1

Happy Day 1 to me. Mum brought me a hot water bottle and a blanket. Dante sat on the sofa too and we watched Horrible Histories together. Dante was fiddling with his willy and mum said, "It's ok to do that, but in private!"

I like to stroke a bit of me that feels really sensitive and nice. I only do that in my room, under the duvet, when I know everyone else is in bed!

In the book my mum gave me, the bit that feels nice and tingly is called the clitoris. It has a hood. That's to protect it because there are so many nerves there. In the book, it says that it's the only part of the body that is only for pleasure. It makes my cheeks go pink when I write that down.

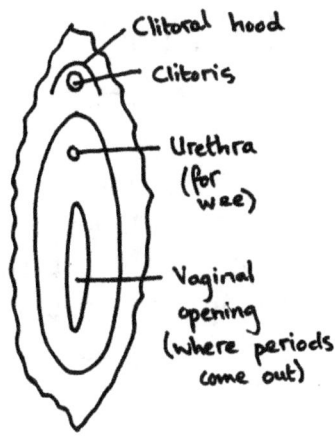

23rd February   DAY 2

I was thinking about Dante fiddling with his willy and I thought it is so easy for boys to see their private parts! Mum gave me a mirror to look at myself a while ago, but I didn't yet. I had a look today and I could see where the blood comes out. There wasn't a lot.

I decided to have a bath because my womb had been achy, and no blood came out at all. I thought maybe the water would turn red! I wonder if I could go swimming without anything?!

24th February DAY 3

Celine came round to my house today. We asked her what she liked to eat and she said pasta so we made it together. She said her dad let her try some wine. She said it was disgusting even when he put water in so that the wine tasted less strong.

28th February DAY 7

We met up with Rose in London for the weekend. I stayed with Rose in her room and she got her period. It came a bit early and she asked me if I had anything with me, but because I just finished my period, I decided not to bring anything to save on space in my suitcase.

She was asking "Why are there bottles of shampoo, and little soaps to use in hotels, but no menstrual products when you need them?" She stuffed toilet paper in her pants and went to the toilets near reception because she thought there might be those machines that sell them, but there weren't any. Then she said she went to the reception to ask for spares, but they didn't have any either.

So in the end mum went to the nearest shop and got some. Rose had asked her to buy extra and she gave those to the lady on the reception desk for future emergencies!! Then we went out for dinner.

We're going to see Matilda at the theatre tomorrow. I can't wait.

1st March DAY 8

Today we find out which secondary school I'll go to. Mum and I woke up early and went downstairs to log onto the computer to see if we could see, but it wasn't up yet. Or at least we couldn't log on – maybe everyone else is trying to see too, at 6.30 in the morning!! I'm so nervous and excited. I hope it's the same as the two Beths and Celine. I'll come back later and let you know dear Diary.

I'm so sad and angry and mad. I didn't get into the school that was my first choice. One of the Beth's is going and Celine. It's totally not fair. I don't want to write any more. IT'S NOT FAIR!

2nd March DAY 9

Yesterday I was so shocked when I didn't get in. My mum said that there's a lot of competition to get a place at that school, but I thought I could do it. I feel stupid or something. But my teacher said I'm clever, and my mum and dad say I'm clever so I feel confused too. Beth One that got into the school said we'll always be friends. I'm worried she'll forget me when she's busy with her new friends.

I spoke to Beth Two and she said she was so happy that we'd be together. That made me feel a bit better. I liked both schools when we went to the open days, but the four of us had decided that we'd go to the girls' school together. It's not my period, but mum said she'd make my favourite dinner anyway!

3rd March DAY 10

The Year 6 had a special assembly today to talk about secondary school places. Some kids didn't get into their first choice but were given a school place for somewhere on the other side of the town. They said it would take two buses to get there! The headteacher said that some of us might feel disappointed, but we all have so much growing up to do and there's plenty of time to show what we can do. Sometimes he can be quite strict, but he was very nice today.

2nd April   DAY 1

40 days! I haven't had a cycle this long for ages. Mum said maybe it was because I was upset about the schools and that delayed my period coming.

8th April   DAY 7

The Easter holidays are starting tomorrow so I made cakes for my friends. I made chocolate crunchy nests and then put little chocolate eggs on top. To make them a bit different, I made chocolate chicks too using a mould my mum got. They looked really good. They TASTED good!

A few days ago, I had no energy to make them, but suddenly today on Day 7 I could feel lots of energy. I looked back at the sheet mum gave me and it said Inner Spring has started. Lucky for my friends!

12th April

Dusty my kitten brought in a dead baby squirrel today. He left it in the kitchen and it looked so little. Dante and I decided to dig a little hole for it in the garden. Mum says that he was leaving it as a present for us, but I wish he wouldn't catch things.

23rd July

I haven't written for months! It's been so busy with Leavers stuff. We had hoodies printed with our names on, and a goodbye picnic and loads of things. The weather's been really nice, so we've been meeting up lots outside.

Today we had the sex talk at school! On the second to last day! The girls and boys went in different rooms and we watched a video. It was a bit old fashioned – the people on the video had funny haircuts and clothes that aren't fashionable now. There was one bit where the penis stands up and everyone laughed.

There wasn't much about periods and I already knew the stuff they talked about. It was a bit rubbish for me that there were only teaching this now. My friend who's at a different primary school said a double decker bus visited their school in Year 6 with lots of stuff to look at inside about periods and bodies.

24th July

Last day of primary school EVER! School finished at 1.30 and we went to the park for a big picnic. Some of the girls were crying because they were moving out of the area or going to different schools. Beth One, Beth Two, Celine and me promised to be good friends.

1st August DAY 1

I haven't written for a few days, but I write the day of my cycle in red ink on the family calendar in the kitchen. No-one's ever asked what the red numbers are!

2nd August DAY 2

Mum got me a teen menstrual cup. It's orange. Because I'm so used to using tampons when I go swimming, she asked "Did I want to try a cup?" I said I'd try because it would be good for when we go on holiday. Yesterday I had to practice folding it in half to be able to fit it in and the cup kept popping open. I got annoyed so I just used a tampon.

Today I had another go. The trick is squatting down. I managed to put it inside like a tampon and then it's like I could feel it open inside. When it's open, nothing can leak out. Once it was in, I could feel it scratching a bit, so mum said to take it out. I washed it and gave it to my mum when I came out of the bathroom. She cut off the stalk underneath the cup so there was nothing scratchy. I was worried about getting it out again because a tampon has a string, but she said I can squeeze my muscles inside and reach it that way. I tried again and it felt much better without the stalk. I went to the beach with it in and couldn't feel it inside at all.

3rd August DAY 3

Today I used the cup again, but as I was taking it out at the end of the day, it fell out of my hand and went all over the floor! I guess I need to practise a bit more. Mum said it's happened to her a number of times, so I didn't feel so bad. Practise makes perfect! Like my diving teacher says every class.

4th August DAY 4

It's getting easier and easier to use the cup, but today we went to visit a museum and there were separate cubicles for the toilet with no sink in the cubicle. I didn't know how I was going to empty the cup out and then clean my hands. Luckily mum was in the ladies too and she guessed the problem. She passed a bottle of water under the door and then I was able to pour the blood in the toilet, wash out the cup and then wash my hands over the toilet! It was a bit tricky but I still like the cup. It's meant to last 10 years! That's as old as me. Just think how many tampons I would use in that time. It would be so good for the environment if I can just get the hang of it.

1st September

Everything's ready for school. I went shopping with mum to get all the uniform: navy skirt, navy jumper with gold stripe around the V neck, white shirt, black tights and shoes. It's very smart but the jumper's a bit itchy. As usual we had to get a size bigger because the size for my age didn't fit me (across my boobs). I've got a new rucksack and pencil case. I've got my old pencil case with my period stuff in.

I wonder what it will be like to have my period at secondary school? I remember from the open day that the toilets were in a different place from the classrooms. I hope I find my way round! I went to the toilet when I went to the open day and the cubicle I went in had a bin for putting pads and tampons in. Much better than my old school. There was also a place to get tampons on the wall. What happens if you don't have the right change?

2nd September

I practiced getting the bus with mum today. I could walk but it would take me 40 minutes! I've got a bus pass with my photo on. It's a really BAD photo. I'm not really smiling and I'm not serious. I've got a huge spot on my chin. Mum says you can't see it on the photo, but I can, and I have to keep the pass for one whole year!

It was really easy getting the bus, but maybe it will be

busier when the holidays end. I was worried about getting off at the right place but there's a petrol station just before my stop so that will remind me. I'm hoping that there'll be other kids from the school on the bus and I can copy them.

Dante came with us on the bus. He wanted to sit at the top at the front of course, but there were some people there already. While we were in town we went to a café. I had my favourite tuna sandwich, but he got a cake and then decided he didn't like it and was grumpy all the way home even when he got to sit at the front of the bus.

3rd September

FIRST DAY! I'm in Miss Nelson's class: 1A. She seems nice but strict! She's a history teacher. I met some new girls who were really friendly. They're called Lucy and Lisa. Lucy looks a bit like me – I mean she's already got boobs. She's really smiley and chatty. Lisa has an older brother in the school. She knew lots of stuff about the teachers from her brother. Her brother said Miss Nelson gives good marks compared to the other history teacher who always writes lots of comments all over your work.

Beth Two is in another class so I only saw her at lunchtime. We ate our packed lunches together and I felt I could relax with her because I've known her for years. I wonder how Beth One and Celine are getting on at the other school?

6th September

We had our first PE lesson today. We got changed and then had to sit on the gym floor while the PE teacher checked our feet for verucas! It was weird. Nobody had one. What would they do if they did find one?! Anyway, while I was sitting there waiting, the girl next to me (Sarah I think) said "You've got hairy legs"!!! To me! I looked at her legs and she didn't have any hair on her legs at all. I looked at the girl who was sitting on the other side of me and she didn't have any hair on her legs. The girl after that did though. Was I meant to have shaved my legs?!

In the morning I'm going to have a look at mum's razor. Maybe I can use that!

7th September

I had a look at mum and dad's razors. I had a little try with mum's, on the bottom of my leg, but I was afraid of cutting myself. I'm going to ask Rose what she does.

8th September DAY 1

My first period at secondary school. It started this morning. I checked I had all my stuff with me in my bag. I decided to wear period pants and I've got a spare pair in case I need to change them. I don't want to have to use the vending machine for a pad in the toilets. It would be embarrassing if someone came in and you couldn't work out how to put your money in or get the pad out!

9th September DAY 2

Today was my heavy flow day. I was really aching when I walked for the bus and I've already got a heavy rucksack of books to carry even though school just started. Mum said I didn't have to go if I didn't feel like it and I must be so tired from starting at the new school, with learning how to get around and all the new faces. I don't want to miss what's happening though – it's like we're still working out who's going to be friends with who.

After lunch, my science teacher Mrs Swann, said I looked a bit pale and was I ok? I didn't want to say I was on my period. It felt like a private thing to say when I've only seen her twice in my whole life. Instead, I said I had a headache. She said "Do you want to go to see the school nurse?" and I said "No, it would be ok". I couldn't really concentrate though and just felt so tired through the afternoon lessons. I'll have to check with Lucy if I missed anything important.

I wore my cup and a pad to be on the safe side. No leaks 😊

When I got home, mum tucked me up with a blanket and hot water bottle on the sofa. It was so lovely to be cosy that I started crying when she went out the room. I wasn't sad, just happy I could relax at last.

Mum came and sat with a cup of tea next to me on the sofa. I said that I thought it would be hard to have to work when you had your period and weren't feeling well. She said yes it could be hard. Luckily she'd not had much pain or heavy flow with her periods, but her aunty had regularly fainted when she had hers in her twenties!

Mum said some women work in a place where they

have something called a Menstrual Policy. The Policy supports women who don't feel well when they have their periods. They can work at home or go home and catch up on the work later. I wish we could do that at school, but I feel like the teachers wouldn't like it or the other girls might think you were being lazy.

But what about if you're a surgeon in the middle of a big operation? You couldn't just stop and leave the patient! Or a policewoman in the middle of arresting someone? "Stay right there, burglar! I just have to go and get a hot water bottle for my cramps." Yeah right. Women have to put up with a lot. I wish people would just speak about it more. That would make it a lot easier.

10th September DAY 3

Today I was changing my period pants in the toilet. It was breaktime so it was busy in the toilets. Someone said "Hurry up! What are you doing in there!". It was so embarrassing! I quickly finished putting on a clean pair of period pants and did up my bag and rushed out, only to see that she was talking to a different cubicle door. I'd rushed for nothing.

I suddenly thought about my mum saying you have to be able to relax to pull a tampon out. I thought it's not very relaxing having your friend outside saying to hurry up. I hope she wasn't trying to do that!!

11th September DAY 4

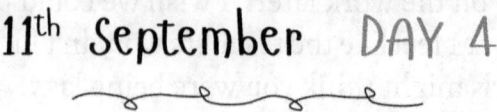

I was telling Rose on the phone about what happened yesterday, and she said she was once in a museum. She went to the toilet and there were four cubicles. As she was having a wee, a child with his mum in the next cubicle said, "What's that?" in a really loud voice. The mum said quietly (but Rose could still hear) "It's my period". The boy shouted, "What's a period?". The mum whispered something, but Rose couldn't hear what she said. The boy said loudly "But why is blood coming out of your bottom"! At this point I was rolling around on my bed laughing and Rose was laughing too.

I guess stuff like this can be embarrassing at the time but is REALLY funny later.

17th September DAY 10

We've had all the teachers now. The maths teacher is my favourite – he tells jokes. The French teacher seems really strict. She gave us so much homework. Rose says she can't really help me with French homework, but she could with Italian! There's no Italian class at school though.

19th September   DAY 12

I had a nosebleed in the middle of French today! Madame Beauvoir held my chin up because she said that it would stop the bleeding, but it made me feel really sick. I asked her if I could go to the toilet to wash the blood off and just let it drip into the basin until it stopped. That was much better. Afterall, I'm an expert with blood!!

26th September   DAY 19

I had to go to the doctor with my mum today. I had an itchy vulva. I couldn't sit still at school. The doctor said I had vaginitis. She thinks it was the bubble bath that I use because I already have cotton knickers that let the air "circulate"!! I totally cringed when the doctor said "circulate" like I had a fan in my knickers. She said that it's best to use something more gentle or natural. I will be so happy when it stops itching. Argghhhh! Mum and I read about it on the Internet and it says water is enough to wash your vulva and you definitely don't want to use anything inside.

2nd October DAY 26

It was Lisa's birthday today. I made cupcakes to take into school because I couldn't take a whole cake on the bus. I knew she liked chocolate and strawberries, so I made chocolate cupcakes with chocolate chips in with a strawberry frosting. My friends were really impressed. It felt so nice to surprise Lisa. It wasn't like at primary school where the whole class sings happy birthday to you, so I was happy that I had the idea to take the cakes in.

Not long until my birthday!

9th October DAY 1

I started swimming club at school. It's really good using the period cup because I don't have to think about changing it during the lesson.

6
Rollercoaster feelings

15th October DAY 7

Mum and dad said they had some big news for us. We sat down at the kitchen table and they said that we're moving house. I was really shocked! I've always lived in this house and Dante was born here. I like my room and Beth One lives just around the corner (now that she's at a different school we see each other at the weekend). We asked where we're moving to and dad said, "Don't worry, not far". I'll still go to the same school.

We're going to see the house that they like tomorrow. Apparently, it's a bit bigger and there will be a spare bedroom and more space downstairs. I just don't want to leave our house. I like it when we've been away to grandma and grandpa's, or away on holiday, and then we turn into our road and see the trees. In the new house we'll be out of town, more in the countryside.

Mum will need to drive me to the bus stop!

I feel really sad. Dad looked disappointed like he thought I'd be so excited and then I wasn't.

16th October DAY 8

We saw the new house and it was quite nice. It has a big kitchen with an island in the middle. Not an island with the sea around, but a counter in the middle of the floor. I can imagine baking there!

Dante and I were fighting over who would have which bedroom, but I couldn't stop thinking about the one I have now. Mum said we can use my design with the rose gold colour on one wall and get the cushions I was thinking about, but I said it wouldn't be the same. I stomped down the stairs and sat down on a step in the garden for ages. I know she was trying to be kind, but she doesn't know how I feel. We've ALWAYS lived in the yellow house.

We're moving in half term! I can't believe it's so close. It's already been decided.

31st October DAY 23

I'm 12! I like being one of the oldest in the year. At the weekend I'm going to the cinema with Beth One, Beth Two, Celine, Emily, Lisa and Lucy. (And my mum!) I didn't think mum would let me bring so many friends, but she says it's a special time because of just starting the new school and having old friends somewhere else. I thought about asking Celine if her older brother would come, but that would be embarrassing haha.

I can't wait to find out how Beth One and Celine are getting on.

1st Nov DAY 24

Yesterday we went to the cinema in the afternoon. The big surprise was that Rose was there too! She didn't meet us at home, but at the cinema. There was this lady walking towards us with massive boxes of popcorn in front of her face. I thought she was going to bang into me, but then she showed her face and it was Rose! She's staying for the whole of half term holidays while we move.

Beth One gave me bath bombs, Beth Two gave me

these really cool star shaped silicone baking cases (so I could make her nice birthday cupcakes wink wink), Celine gave me a book called Reaching for the Moon (I peaked and it looks like it's about periods – her mum gave one to her and she thought I'd like it too!), Emily forgot to bring my present so her mum's going to post it, Lisa gave me a notepad with this sequin cover and Lucy gave me a cool T-shirt.

Beth One and Celine said they had loads of homework. We do at my school too. It didn't sound so different.

I made a cake to have when we got home. I decided on a three-tier cake with strawberries in between each layer. I did it all myself except for the cream that mum helped me with. I thought it looked very grownup. Dante said his treasure chest cake was much better!

He gave me one of his lego figures, which I know is very special to him, and a big hug. He's very sweet and a great brother really.

Today Rose helped me pack things into boxes. I still feel really sad about moving. Who's going to be living in the house when we've moved? Who will have my room? Mum says a family with a baby is coming to live there. She's they seem very nice and will look after the house well. But who cares!

Mum and Dad gave me some money for my birthday this year so I can choose things to put in my new room. Rose is going shopping with me tomorrow to help choose. I'm excited to go on a shopping spree.

Mum looked alarmed when I said "Shopping <u>spree</u>"! I know I'm going to buy a new duvet cover that matches my colour theme and cushions. I hope I can find what I want.

3rd November   DAY 26

Everything's packed up that can be. Just my sleeping things to put in a big bag for the new house tomorrow. I'm saving my new duvet for when we've painted my new room. Mum already got the paint ready. I think she knows how sad I've been feeling and is trying to cheer me up.

4th November   DAY 27

I'm writing this in my new bedroom.   It feels very weird.

6th November   DAY 29

Dusty's gone missing. Mum says he's probably just

exploring the new area, but she looked a bit worried. Dad, Rose and I painted my room – it looks really good. Beth Two is coming tomorrow.

7th November   DAY 30

Beth Two came and she really liked my room. We sat in the garden for ages chatting and calling for Dusty. Then she said she heard from her brother (who's friends with Beth One's brother) that Beth One is having her birthday party next weekend. I haven't had an invitation, so I guess I'm not invited. I feel sad that she came to the cinema for my birthday and she's not invited me for hers. I feel left out.

17th November   DAY 40

Still no period and I've been feeling stressed out. There's so much homework and it's horrible standing in the rain waiting for the bus to arrive at my new bus stop. I didn't want to get out of the car this morning when mum was dropping me off. She said "I know it's hard moving to a new house. What can we do to help?" I said "I hate you and I wish we never moved from the old house. You only think about yourself." I feel REALLY bad now.

28th November DAY 51
turned into Day 1

Day 1. I've been waiting so long for this period and now it's really hurting. It's only Day 1 and there's more blood than normal. Luckily, it's Saturday and I can just snuggle on the sofa.

29th November DAY 2

Really tired and slept to 10 o'clock! Which I never do. I had to take a paracetamol for the first time for period pain.

OWWWWWWWWWWWWWWWWWW!

Mum said maybe it's because I've been feeling sad about leaving the old house, worried about Dusty who's not come back, stressed about the new school and more homework, and stressed about Beth 1 not inviting me to her party or her house. She said that's a lot!

30th November — DAY 3

I had to take a day off school today. I was crying when mum said to get dressed in my school uniform. She said "Ok, let's spend the day working out what will help". After we dropped Dante at school, we went and bought a white noise thing. She said she was thinking about getting it for me at Christmas, but that I needed it now. It plays different relaxing sounds like waves, birds tweeting, calm piano music, but my favourite is the rain sound. Plip plop, plip plop. I just love it.

Mum downloaded a relaxation app on the ipad and she said I can listen to it as I fall asleep. We also talked about how she felt hurt when I said "I hate you" to her the other day. I said "Sorry, I didn't mean it." She said she knows that, and it's ok to be angry, but you've got to try not to use mean words or throw things on the floor. I'm going to try going to my room when I feel angry and even maybe try punching the cushion. Then when I've calmed down, she says we can talk, and she can listen to what's worrying me.

I feel better that we've talked about everything.

1st December   DAY 4

There was much less blood today and I felt less tired. I went to school and Lisa said she'd lend her books to me so I could catch up on yesterday's work.

2nd December   DAY 5

Beth Two, Lisa and Lucy are coming for a sleepover at the weekend. Lisa and Lucy haven't seen my room yet.

I couldn't go to sleep yesterday because I was thinking about how long it took to copy out all the work I missed, but I put on the rain drop sound and fell asleep.

5th December   DAY 8

Mum said maybe my period hurt more this time because I've been eating more chocolate and junk food. The week we moved we ate more junky stuff and she said maybe we need get back to a healthier diet. She said she'd do it with me. So for my friends coming I did make some cupcakes, but I also made some healthy cheesy muffins. They were really good! We had popcorn too, but just with salt on. The others hadn't made popcorn before, so we made it in the saucepan and jumped around when it started popping.

6th December   DAY 9

It was so good having my friends around. It made it feel like we haven't moved so far. And big news! Beth Two has started her period. She started last week and was super proud telling me and said her mum had taken her to have her ears pierced this morning to celebrate! She's got normal studs now, but she says her mum gave her some red earrings made from coral for later on.

7th December   DAY 10

Not long until Christmas. Mum says I can have a good rest over the holidays, and I won't be a new girl anymore when I go back in January. She said everything's more tiring when it's new.

17th December   DAY 20

I had my first swimming competition at school today and I came first in the breaststroke. I was so happy that I was in my Inner Autumn because I wouldn't have been able to go as fast during my period (my Inner Winter).

Celine's brother is in the swimming club and he came and said, "Well done" and slapped me on the back!

24th December   DAY 27

We finished school today for the Christmas holidays. We finished at the normal time instead of at 1.30 like at primary school. I thought the afternoon would never end.

I said to mum to just get me a surprise this Christmas.

25th December   DAY 28

We're at home for Christmas and then we're going to grandma and grandpa's for New Year.

We haven't opened our presents yet. Dante is STILL asleep and it's nearly 9am! Argh I can't wait any longer.

We opened our presents after breakfast in the end. One of things mum got me is a diffuser. You can put drops of oils on the water and then it blows out the oil in a kind of steam. It can also change colour if you like. She got me lavender oil and geranium, but she said I can go and choose another essential oil soon. It's really pretty when you turn the big light off on the ceiling and the diffuser changes from green to blue to pink...

Mum and dad also got me a special swimming costume that stops your period coming out when you're in the water! I never heard of them before. I might check it works in the bath first. They said because I'm doing so much swimming it might be helpful.

28th December DAY 31

The best present ever arrived today! Dusty came home!! He looked a bit thinner and was covered in dust and cobwebs. Mum says we'll never know where he's been. I hope he's learned his lesson!

7
My secret superpower

29th December DAY 32

Change of plan! Because Dusty has only just got back home, grandma and grandpa are coming to us instead. I made some of my cheesy muffins for when they arrive. Mum's stopped buying biscuits and crisps so we can be healthier together. She said "Everything in moderation" so we do have some chocolate after dinner!

3rd January DAY 37
turned into Day 1

I had a feeling my period was coming. It didn't come in the morning as it usually does, but in the afternoon. I went to the toilet and thought "Oh hello!".

I'm so happy it wasn't 51 days like last time. Also, it's started more slowly like usual. It's good to get back to normal.

4th January — DAY 2

Mum organised a treat for grandma, her and me. She has a friend who is a reflexologist (a person who massages feet). We set up the lounge like a spa with my diffuser, calm music and lots of cushions. I thought the reflexology would be tickly, but it was really relaxing. I fell asleep at one point.

Dad, grandpa and Dante cooked dinner. It was pasta with garlic bread, and tiramsu for afterwards. It was really good.

5th January — DAY 3

I realised that I didn't have any pain this period. I can see how when I was feeling unhappy and stressed it really affected my body. Mum's reflexologist friend said that the period is like a barometer for how healthy your body is. She explained that a barometer measures the pressure outside and helps forecast the weather, but what I think she meant is that if you have a painful period it shows that there is something going on with how you feel or how healthy your body is.

It's quite useful! If I hadn't had such a painful, heavy period, I might not have talked to my mum about how upset I was feeling. She says the menstrual cycle is women's secret superpower! If you listen to your cycle carefully and look for patterns over the months, it can give us a lot of information back.

6th January DAY 4

Back to school today and it does feel a bit different. I know my way around the corridors, I know the teachers' names and how things work. I feel like I could dive off a very high diving board again!

I've signed up for yoga at school this term. It felt really good when I tried it at home with mum. At least I won't have Dante standing on my hair at school.

10th February DAY 1

It's been over two years since I had my first period. So many things have happened! I finished primary school, moved to a new house, lost and found my cat, lost and found friends. I've tried all sorts of menstrual products and worked out how to deal with different period situations.

Sometimes it was hard having a period, especially when I was one of the first girls in my class, but now I look forward to it starting. I don't want another 51-day cycle though! I'm still using my chart and I know I get spots and get a bit clumsy during my Inner Autumn. I like hot water bottles and blankets on the sofa in my Inner Winter. I start to feel energy again in the Inner Spring. I really like Celine's brother during the Inner Summer. Blush.

I feel like I have a map of what my body's doing and why I might be feeling the way I feel. That makes it a bit less confusing when I feel down or angry.

Before the half term holidays, we're going to raise money for a charity at school. I suggested fundraising for sewing machines to make reusable pads in Kenya, so the girls don't have to miss school. The teachers and other girls really like my idea (the boys not so much) and so they chose the charity I suggested. I feel really proud that I've got the children in my year talking about periods. The swimming club teacher now has a red box, with pads and tampons inside. So girls don't need to worry if they start their periods when they weren't expecting them.

Periods are part of my life. I've made friends with my period. I've filled up this diary, so it's time for a new journal.

Thanks, dear Diary, for being there xx

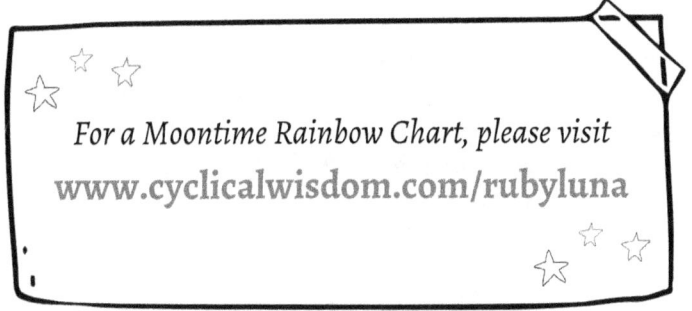

For a Moontime Rainbow Chart, please visit
www.cyclicalwisdom.com/rubyluna

See Tessa's other books...

Ruby Luna's Curious Journey

Go with Ruby Luna on a journey around her body finding out the correct words to speak about her lower anatomy and discovering what is where. The book helps support parents to answer those tricky questions and has multi-cultural, relatable illustrations and fun actions to keep it entertaining. Aimed at 5-10 year olds girls.

Dante Leon's Curious Journey

Follow Dante Leon and his friends on a journey around the male body and how it changes during puberty. In a similar format to Ruby Luna's Curious Journey, the multi-cultural and fun drawings, and crazy facts keep children entertained. Aimed at 7-11 year old boys.

Available on

www.ingramcontent.com/pod-product-compliance
Lightning Source LLC
Chambersburg PA
CBHW070433010526
44118CB00014B/2022